Dorothy Dunnett Society and
Historical Writers' Association

Short Story Competition 2023

Published by the Dorothy Dunnett Society, Edinburgh, and the Historical Writers' Association, London.

The Dorothy Dunnett Society is a Scottish Charitable Incorporated Organization No. SC030649.
The Historical Writers' Assocation is registered in England, number 09132674 at The Union Building, 51-59 Rose Lane, Norwich NR 1 1BY.

First published by the Dorothy Dunnett Society/ Historical Writers' Association in 2023

Dorothy Dunnett Society and
Historical Writers' Association

Short Story Competition 2023

History is all very well but it's just the showcase. It is the arena in which your characters will perform, and which supplies the conflicts, stresses, dilemmas and the struggles they'll get through.

Dorothy Dunnett

CONTENTS

INTRODUCTION

The standard of entries for the Dorothy Dunnett Society and the Historical Writers' Association's Unpublished Short Story Competition of 2023 was higher than ever. Writers everywhere, and at every stage of their career, can learn something from how these shortlisted writers create a world, a period, and full-blooded and full-voiced characters in less than 3500 words as well as stories which subvert our expectations and redeliver us to the modern world with the scents and textures of the past under our fingertips.

We received over a hundred stories again this year. All entries are judged anonymously, and we are very grateful to our first readers for helping us to plunge into this treasure trove to select a longlist of twenty-five. The stories selected for the longlist are all of exceptional quality, and I sincerely hope the longlisted writers will continue to explore historical fiction. Each has obviously found history is fertile ground for fiction, and we hope to see much more of their work in future.

It was a great pleasure to hear our final round judges discussing and debating the longlist, arguing for their favourites, comparing very different styles and periods, people and places, to find the stories which felt to them most complete and impactful. We are very grateful to them for the time and trouble they take to consider the stories so thoughtfully. Each story selected is, we hope you'll agree, imbued with that certain x factor which makes fiction an art as well as a craft. They are to be savoured.

Our winner this year, *Hecate's Daughter* by Jo Tiddy, paints a portrait of a community and landscape which has the watery glow of a Vermeer, but remains rooted in the tangible, textural and historical. The writing is superb, and the voice of the narrator absolutely convincing, creating a piece which combines subtlety and high drama to great effect.

Dawn Rising by Anne Byrne, one of our highly commended stories, is formally daring, but manages to be both lyrical and urgent, bringing intense focus to a small patch of space and time. The snap twist of the ending is delivered with expert precision, and its implications ripple back over the story to giving another, deeper resonance to a work which already moves and convinces. Our second highly commended entry, *Black Christ* by Judith Wilson, uses a first-person narrator to plunge us into the life of a teenager in Liverpool. It's vivid and uncompromising and in creating one work of art from another, fixes both indelibly in the imagination.

The Roaring Girl by Louise Morrish is a delicious monologue, peppery and spiced, which makes creative use of its self-imposed restrictions to bring to life a character both vivid and visceral. *Well Water* by Josie Turner is a perfectly formed slice of gothic Americana, which delivers an ending worthy of Roald Dahl with elegant, deadly restraint. Our final story, *Who Can Believe in Witches* by Cheryl Burman, is a superbly satisfying work, both lyrical and unsettling, which sets off all manner of echoes and resonances and revels in the passing on of hidden traditions and esoteric knowledge.

We are proud and delighted to share these stories and writers with you.

Imogen Robertson, Chair, HWA

WINNER
Jo Tiddy

About the Author

Jo grew up in Africa and moved back to the UK to complete her education. After completing a degree at Sheffield University, she reluctantly accepted that she needed to get a proper job. Postgraduate degrees from UWE and Oxford Brookes followed. For over twenty years Jo was a town planner and historic buildings officer in local government, which gave her an abiding love of history and a mild aversion to bureaucracy. Ten years ago she became a bookseller in a fantastic independent bookshop in Thame and finally found her calling.

Her adult short stories have won at Henley, Thame, and Norwich Writers competitions. She has been variously long or shortlisted for Exeter, Wells, Bristol, Bath, Yeovil, Frome, and Mslexia magazine competitions. She was a finalist in the 2022 Exeter Novel Prize.

Jo has written three (as yet unpublished) historical novels for young adults and is represented by Penny at Holroyde Cartey. She is currently working on a novel set in AD61 and is preparing to raze Colchester to the ground…

Jo is also a garden designer, dog whisperer, and

crochet addict, and is occasionally found swimming in the Thames or on the Norfolk coast depending on the temperature. She lives in rural Buckinghamshire, not far from the dreaming spires of Oxford, and when not selling books she can be found scribbling in her shed, planting bulbs, and wondering what her children are getting up to, now that they have finally left home.

She can be found lurking mostly on Instagram @jo_tiddy.

HECATE'S DAUGHTER

By Jo Tiddy

She brings me breakfast, the sour-faced woman who keeps house here, slamming it on the table. She don't speak. A hunk of bread, a bowl of milk. Dinner is pottage. It looks and tastes like dishwater. I dream of sharp green apples, of samphire, of summer-ripe hedgefruit. I dream of flying through the narrow window and across the northern sea to the Low Countries, where it is said that they are kinder to children.

'What have I done?' The words skitter, trapped mice in my head. They don't come out.

She won't say, not her. Just throws me a hard look and locks the door behind her. A prison then, this sober room at the top of the wool-stapler's house. It's a big house; it smells of wood-smoke and money. I look out from the garret: at the port, the channel through the patchwork marshes. The wide blue freedom beyond them. I see the ships waiting to escape. I won't look south towards the church, or the boneyard filled with the dead. There's a jug of water left always on the table, but I don't touch it.

Last summer the Sweat took off a load of the villagers.

It comes through most years when the haymaking's done and it leaves orphans in its wake. Had the village scared. Folk murmured it was because the king had put aside his wife to marry that Bullen witch. Our priest called it a judgement from God, because of the wickedness of certain inhabitants.

'Suffer the little children, and forbid them not....'
The priest was sermonising every Sunday. Other banalities which mean nowt to those most in need, especially the littlest. Those who are just mouths to feed. The villagers looked at each other. Looked at me, sideways. Did nothing. Those children ended up at Binham, at Weybourne, as servants of the church. It's a hard childhood, scrubbing away the sins of the Fathers.

They tell me I was lucky, because when Ma died the baker took me in.

'It's my Christian duty,' he said as he eyed me up and down, like I was a cull-ewe at market. Said I could help out around the house. His wife, all la-di-da, don't like getting her hands dirty. Sat all day in her front room, she was, sewing and chatting with the other merchant-wives grown fat on wool profits. I had one meal a day and a pallet in the bake house. It was close to the ovens so at least it was warm. It wasn't too long before the baker came visiting at night.

'I need the comfort,' he said. Didn't feel real comfortable to me. His hands were rough, scabbed by bake-fires. His mouth, in the dark, stank of rot.

'Don't say a word." He'd pinch my cheek hard when he left. He knew I don't speak. He must have said something though, because the priest came too, sometimes, in the blackest hours of the night, when only Hecate is wakeful. He'd make the sign of the cross above me.

'Jesus loves you and will forgive your sin.' He wouldn't look at me while he fumbled away. Face and hair of flame, sweating. Afterwards he would pray, words running out like tears. He'd haul me up beside him to share out his sin. The kneeling on the cold floor was worse than the fumbling. It certainly went on for longer.

Now it's February, and my belly is big. Feels like I've swallowed a serpent. When the baker's wife finds out she goes mad. Howling and screeching, as if possessed by a demon. Baker says nothing, just slid his eyes away, from his wife, from me, from the pious neighbours who hide their smiles behind their hands. I'm hauled before the elders who poke away with their questions. I say nothing, but then I never had words. That's why Ma kept me close, away from the village kids and their cruel taunts. Most people would have put me out on the heath to die, but Ma would never snuff out a child of her own body. That other women would did not concern her.

'You are precious,' she'd say. 'You are beloved.' She'd kiss me and set me running up on the high heath where the air was clear. Up near the gallows, where the memories of long-dead witches linger, living on the dead ground of flint and sand. No one sees them but me. It's no place for a child to run wild but I like it up there, with just the curlews and the silent witches for company.

Now I am no longer free to wander. The elders lock me

up, for my own safety, they say. They suggest that I'm not right in the head, that I cannot be allowed to roam, a temptress loose.

'A viper nourished at my bosom, more like!' says the baker's wife, chins wobbling with righteousness. The baker keeps his mouth tight shut, and doesn't dare to look at his wife.

Priest comes by day, now I'm locked up, telling me to repent. He does it loudly, so the folk in the downstairs rooms can hear him. I don't know what he's talking about, I just shake my head at him, give him a hard stare. He knows he won't get a confession. He looks everywhere except my face. He looks frightened, and I like that. It sustains me during the long and mercifully lonesome nights. The dawns arrive; again, again, again. I look out of the window and dream of sea storms.

Three years ago the sea rose and took Pa. 'Twas a storm called up by a witch!' folk say still, as if they haven't got enough troubles in the here and now to be thinking of. Always harking back to the past. Always remembering wrongs from long ago. But that storm, it was something to remember. The wind howled in from the north and drove the waves over the shingle bank that separates marsh from sea. It flooded us out. Big skies meeting endless sea, and only the shingle to protect us. The boats in the harbour were smashed to kindling, the houses drowned. Many died, swept away by the wild waves or tugged underwater by new and treacherous currents. Pa, out on the boat, was lost. I dream of it sometimes. And I dream I'm flying free over the marshes, away. Me, who has never been much further than Salthouse. They have the higher ground, and a big church set into the side of the heath. It's closer to heaven, they reckon. Pa washed up there and we went to collect his body from the shore and carted it back to a pauper's grave here in Cley. Once he'd been tamped into the ground, snug-like, Ma had asked our priest if he would say some prayers, and he had laughed in her face.

'No coin, no prayers.'

Ma strode away, dragging me with her, though I'd wanted to stay close to Pa for a little while more. Her mouth was tight, her voice fury.

'Piss on all churchmen.'

When he came to our cottage on the heath edge later, she didn't turn him away. He sidled up like a fox at dusk.

'Go and gather ransomes,' said Ma, and her eyes said, don't argue, even though the wild garlic grows only in Kelling Wood and it would be dark before I got home. When I got back the priest was gone, and Ma was wrapping up her hair into its heavy coil. Pa was mentioned in prayers that week, and the weeks after. Where she got the coin from I don't know.

It wasn't the Sweat what did for Ma. She died from pushing out a baby. I was there, frightened silly by the screams and the muck. I wrapped the bairn up real tight, covering its hair so no-one would see. It were dead anyway. Then I ran for help. Ma wouldn't stop bleeding. Midwife came, took one look and shook her head. Then she went back to the village, gossiping and spreading ill-will. Ma, with her last breath, said to me, 'Watch that red-haired devil.' She never warned about the baker. I had to learn that for myself.

The villagers took to muttering. Ma was a wise woman, good with herbs and potions. She'd let me help, with the picking and the drying and the pounding together of bits of this and that. The goodwives of the village were happy enough to creep up to our cottage with their ailments, or when they needed a child loosening, or a love potion. When she died of the bairn though they said 'Witch,' and looked sideways at their husbands. Nobody admitted to the baby, and they buried them both outside the churchyard, with the unbaptized and the bastards. Tossed them in a hole in the ley, with not a single prayer. The priest sermonised about Jezebel, about harlots, and the weakness of Eve. The women of the parish looked at me and made the sign of the horns.

Now my stomach hurts. My back hurts. I want to scream, but the screaming won't come out. Suddenly there are women here, all crowding round me. Goodwives from the village. The useless midwife who wouldn't save Ma. All here to help, they say, all here to witness my humiliation.

'Hold her down,' says the midwife, as I endure, and their hot hands are on me, pinching, leaning over me so I cannot breathe, cannot do anything to prevent the flood of tears that accompanies the pain.

'These are the wages of sin," says one of the women, crossing herself. She can talk, sanctimonious cow. Her brats who look nothing like their father, or each other. I seen her walking out at nights, with other folk's husbands while her own is out on the boats.

'She didn't sin by herself,' says another, darkly, and she squeezes my hand, which for a moment, is comfort. The midwife spits, turns away. She's not interested in measuring out blame. A crest of pain, and I think I must die, and I squeeze my eyes shut and plead silently for God's forgiveness.

When the baby comes they examine her for signs of deformity, for signs of the Devil. They see her flaming red hair and exchange sly looks. One, kinder, shows me how to give suck, cleans me up, combs out my hair. She hums a quiet tune under her breath as she does so, and slowly I come back to calmness.

'You must eat, child,' she says. 'You need your strength for the babe.' She hands me an apple from her pocket. 'I will bring more,' she promises. She lays a hand on the baby's head, a benediction of sorts. Then they leave us alone.

The thing is, I know more than they think. They think I am simple, but I understand plenty. I see things enfolded in people's hearts, dark things, hidden things. I hear snatches of conversation as if carried by the breeze. I get a feel for what people are thinking. The voices of the goodwives whisper along the wainscoting; they murmur that the King's Men are up and down this coast, looking for wickedness, carrying out inspections; churches, priories, and abbeys. The House of the Lord stands on shifting sands these days, and change is coming. There's a lot I could tell them, if I only had the words. Would they even listen?

Time passes. I dream of storm clouds rising, of a

Queen falling. They leave me and the bairn alone, except for feeding. Don't let us go. Strange men in rich clothes come. They huff and puff up the narrow stairs and gaze at me from the safety of the doorway. These are the men sent by the King, to inspect, to judge, it appears, me.

'The girl is a fool.' I hear one mutter. 'Can we burn a fool?' Another is thinking only of his dinner, of roast capons and suckling pig, of a good Rhenish to wash it down.

'You'll get no sense from her,' says the woman who brings me apples. 'She has no words.' She means it kindly enough. She pats the baby's cheek and smiles at me. 'Pretty child,' she says. It is not enough.

They load me onto a cart one cheerless Saturday. I clutch my baby girl tight, swaddled and wrapped. Apple woman has unbound my hair and it flows darkly down my back. She weeps as she grasps my hands. 'God bless you.' Then she is gone, swallowed up by the tide of people that line the quayside. I hope she runs far away from what's coming. The cart follows the procession of churchmen down the street. We roll down to the green, beside the church, the chantry chapels bestowed by wealthy woolmen. 'God loves a cheerful giver,' they think, as if money, hard coin, could save their souls. I see it clearly, our glorious church, blasted and roofless in times to come.

The people press closer. There are more of them crowding the green. Strangers. They must have come from Blakeney, from Wiveton, lured by the promise of a spectacle, a good day out. Though I think that the folk I have known my whole life are strangers now. I see the stake, pointing to heaven, I see the wood piled around it. I see the plush King's Men ranged like holy statutes in front of the churchyard wall. 'Witch, Devil's spawn,' the people call out as I pass. God ripples away from them like a breeze across the barley field.

A rough rope is looped around my waist to fix me to the stake. They uncover my child and bind her to me. I see the devil, genuflecting before me. I see him looking at our daughter, with her flame-red hair, and I bare my teeth at him as his pale face gets whiter and he tries to reach for her.

The crowd roars. It's an animal in pain, a wave of noise. They drag the priest away, and someone tosses a flaming brand onto the kindling. The fire is set. Heat tickles my toes and smoke curls ups like a snake. I turn my head and feel the rage begin to burn in my breast.

Finally, at last, I find my voice. After these years of silence, the words fill me like holy water into an empty vessel.

'Oh! Great Worm!' I howl. 'Oh! Demons of Hell. He had my mother. He had me!' I point at the priest, cursing. I catch sight of the baker, shimmering through the rising smoke haze. 'And him too!' Baker is shuffling backwards through the throng fast as he can. He knows too well the memory of fire, of skin blistered by hot coals. The goodwives of the village stop him. They pen him, pinch and pummel him. He'll get what's coming to him. Priest will too, he's being bundled up and dragged towards the King's Men. Maybe they'll burn him. I hope they burn him.

'I call on you, Oh Satan. Avenge your daughter!' The crowd are shifting backwards, silent now. I laugh at them. 'Your churches will fall. Your children will shrivel in the womb. Your kine will drown and your harvest will rot. Your ships will die on the waves and your sons will choke on the salt waters.' Flames rise. Like a holy miracle the rope that ties me to the post falls away, and we are flying, sky-borne, my baby and I, out across the marshes, out across the rising waves. I look down at the smudge of smoke, at folk scattering like foolish chickens when the fox gets in, and I scream with joy. I call up a witch's wind. I raise a storm.

About the Author

Anne Byrne lives in rural County Sligo, Ireland, a rugged and historic landscape that inspires her writing. Being an avid reader and history enthusiast from an early age she always harboured an ambition to write historical fiction. She recalls her first library loan at an age when she couldn't even see above the counter as *Myths and Legends of Ancient Ireland* and from here on she was hooked on historical fiction.

Always with a book in her hand, and another on stand-by just in case, it was the milestone of turning forty in 2016 that finally prompted her to put pen to paper (or fingers to keyboard) in pursuit of her writing ambitions. Making a start on the novel that had plagued her for years she was tempted away by a local short story competition, writing her first short story in 2017. Though unsuccessful in the competition, she carried on writing short fiction and was rewarded with a second placing in the same competition, the Roscommon New Writing Award, the following year. Since this she has been short and longlisted in various competitions including the Kanturk Flash Fiction Competition 2019, the Anthology Short Story Competition 2021 and the Fish Flash Fiction Competition 2021, while placing third in the Allingham Flash Fiction Competition 2021 and the Bard of Connacht Poetry Competition 2022. She was both shortlisted and overall winner of the Roscommon New Writing Award 2020.

Anne was the recipient of the Roscommon Chapbook Bursary Award 2021 resulting in the publication of her first collection of historical short fiction, *The Bottom of the Hourglass,* later that same year.

She has recently returned to her novel and the world of 11th-century warring Irish kings where she hopes to remain until the war is finally won.

Find her on X @atwbyrne and on Facebook @annebyrnewriter.

DAWN RISING

By Anne Byrne

Kilmainham Gaol, Dublin, Ireland,
1916

You imagine that the birds are singing and that the sky has returned to its near-summer shade of pale washed blue, that you are at home, beneath the gentle sweep of the sycamores, that there has been no smoke, no rubble, no blood upon the streets of Dublin, that the flag you fashioned from an old bedspread still hangs proud above the General Post Office.

Beneath you the hard stone of the floor breathes its dampness into your bones, seeping through the thin weave of the grain sack. You shift onto your side, pull your knees into your chest, clamp your hands so tight against your ears it hurts.

You try not to think who's out there, beyond the small window. You know that if you stand on the copper piping along the wall, you can stretch yourself just enough to see.

You remember how your toes trembled, how your fingers clung to the sharp edge of the sill, how you'd strained yourself towards the sky, the soft semblance of air upon your skin; how you'd fallen away as the shots rang out, toes crumbling like twigs beneath you, the flesh of your fingers leaking scraps of blood onto the blackened stone.

This morning you'd woken again before the dawn, the patch of window still black, surprised that sleep had taken you so easily. You'd lain there, heart clamouring in your chest, the ghost of some nightmare at your back. There was a stillness to the place, as though the world had paused for breath, and you waited with it, refusing for a moment to suck in the dank, stale air, the smell of your own piss in the bucket beside you. As you stole a breath, it was as if the place itself breathed with you, slowly stirring to life; somewhere the clang of a door, a murmur of voices drifting through the thinning dark. You'd blessed yourself then, clutching for the tiny crucifix about your neck, pressing its cold, hard body to your broken lips.

The first crack of gunfire comes in the murk of early light. You try not to hear it, keeping your world tightly closed within the seal of your splayed palms, but it whips itself into your brain. You curl tighter into yourself, but it comes again...and again...and again.

Four, you count, your body rocking to its own beat...*four*...The echoes shrivel and die at last. *Four*, you whisper, faces coming at you in a flicker of guilt as you open your ears, letting your hands fall loosely where they will. You turn onto your back, your bones shrieking within you.

There are scratchings on the far wall, like old scars, white against the mottled flesh of the stone. You feel the rise and fall of yourself, the leather buttons, like pebbles beneath your fingers. You pull on one, worrying it loose like a bad tooth.

When you try to stand your legs give way, and you buckle like a foal. You try again, edging yourself up the wall until you are pressed flat against it. The smell makes you push away, reminding yourself of your own filth. The scars are clearer now, some fresh, and you wonder who was here before you.

You find a spot, midway down the wall. The leather bites into the grime, and you scratch it away, wearing yourself slowly into the skin of stone, dust falling upon dust, bits of it sparkling in the tiny scrap of sun that has somehow found its way into the smallness of your space to catch this one single moment of forever.

The sun has left you by the time your door rattles for breakfast. You have no stomach for it, pushing the bread away, into the corner with last night's bully beef. The water is stale, with a tang of warmth about it that makes you retch. Still, you drink it down, hoping it might soften the crumpled bag of your tongue.

They come for you shortly afterwards. You stand, pulling your jacket straight, wishing now that you hadn't had to sacrifice your button, for its absence makes a gap, puckering the fabric outwards when you move. You just have time to grab your hat as they pull you roughly towards the door.

You know you're going to die like the rest of them.

The guards say nothing as they return you to your cell. You sit at the table, hoping that the bit of candle will be enough. You're not sure what to write, or who to write it to. You try a poem, but when you read it back it sings of despair. You push it away, rise, pace the tiny floor. In the corner things move across the sheen of the discarded bully beef. A wave of nausea rips through you, sends you grabbing for the chair.

'Dearest old Darling,' you write, blinking the stars out of your eyes. The page stares back. You slump forward, drop your pen, watch as a blot of ink bleeds onto the paper. You could make it something beautiful if you had the words of Pearse, or Plunkett, or if you had your easel and your paints, but there is only this bruise of blue, this thin strip of dirty white.

The candle splutters, slowly drowning in its own juice. You tip it sideways, gently releasing the molten wax onto the table. You can't help but touch it, watch as your fingers push its edges inwards, making of it something you almost recognise.

You don't feel your fingers burn or the film of it clinging to your skin. You feel nothing for a blessed moment, almost oblivious to the intrusive creak of the door. In a fumble you push the hardened wax away, not caring that it snaps and breaks, leaving little bits of itself behind.

'My child,' you hear. 'I have come to pray with you.' You feel yourself tighten, but you make yourself look up. The prison chaplain is a tall man, thin as a spectre. Yet, he seems to steal the very air away from you.

'Reverend,' you mutter, picking at the hard slick of wax on your finger. 'I'm expecting Father Albert.'

'There might not be time,' he says, dipping his large head as if the sorrow alone is his to bear.

'He'll be here,' you reply. 'Besides, there's been no sentence yet.'

The chaplain closes his eyes, nods his head again. 'We should pray,' he says, clasping his hands together.

'I'll wait for Father Albert,' you say.

'I have others to see,' replies the chaplain, rocking stiffly on the balls of his feet. 'This could be your last chance.'

'I'll wait,' you say again, bending to your page.

The silence stretches, taut as a rope.

'May God go with you then,' he replies, turning away. He stops, one hand on the door. 'Ah, I was told to mention'—he nods towards the crumpled prison uniform on the floor beside your sleeping mat— 'you might want to change…ah…show some remorse perhaps…' He is half-gone, a sliver of shadow in the closing maw of the door, before his words reach you.

'I fought in these clothes,' you shout, rattling from your chair, 'and by God, I'll die in them!' The door clanks shut. Your anger slides miserably against it, drops to the floor.

You never thought a day could take so long to get to the end of itself.

When the small wooden bowl is pushed through the hatch, you almost faint with the relief of it, then pinch yourself so hard you know you'll be as blue as the blot of ink tomorrow.

The stink of stale cabbage wafts its way into your stomach. You take small slurps, feeling the heat of it sink into your bowels.

You think of your sister, Eva, and the letter you need to write. You force a few lines onto the page, leave some space for them to breathe.

The darkness doesn't let you sleep. You hear it move, settle, shift. You feel it match its breath to yours.

You wonder if you'll ever see the stars again.

You scream silently as guns crack the dawn again for the third day.

Words come, falling like tears onto the paper.

You wait for Father Albert.

As you sit together, him perched on the edge of the table, you whisper a silent goodbye to the sun.

He lights a cigarette, takes a long draw, hands it to you. The taste is sweeter than you remember. You suck on it hungrily, watch it burn like the rising dawn, before handing it back.

'Dead,' you repeat, shaking your head. 'I wondered who...but...'

Father Albert nods, exhaling a thin trail of smoke. 'Aye, eight so far, God rest them.
Pat and Willie, Clarke, McDonagh, Plunkett—'

'Christ,' you say, grabbing for the cigarette.

'Aye' he continues. 'Daly, O'Hanrahan...'

You run a hand through your hair, feeling the tangled mess of it.

'...McBride, this morning.'

'Christ,' you whisper again, taking another pull of the cigarette.

'The people are turning though, Con,' says Father Albert. He stops, fumbles for something to say. 'It...it won't be for naught, I promise.' He puts a hand to your shoulder. 'Something's changed...the ordinary people...I don't know, but it looks like things are changing...

they're with ye now…'

You take another drag, hold the cigarette towards him.

'Finish it,' he says, quietly.

You nod your thanks, letting the silence settle between you.

'Will you hear my confession, Father?' you ask at last, flicking the exhausted butt to the floor.

You write some more, on the paper Father Albert has given you, to Joss and Casi, to your daughter Maeve. The candle dies slowly, guttering away to nothing.

There is a slight moon. You catch it for an instant as it rides above the clouds. The stars are meagre things beyond your window, dull as old farthings in the deep pocket of night. You watch as they fade, as a hue of light paints itself across them.

You are still there at the table, in the half-dark, when the guard comes. He bangs in, holds back the door, a lantern held high in his other hand. Another man steps past him. This one is young, barely a whisker to his cheek, the stamp of an officer on his chest. He looks past you, to some spot on the wall perhaps, holds himself tight as a drum, and pretends to read from the sheet of paper in his hand.

'Constance Markievicz,' he declares. 'It has been proven that you did take part in an armed rebellion against His Majesty, the King, and having been tried by Court Martial are found guilty and sentenced to death'—his eyes flick towards you— 'by being shot.'

You bow your head, feel for the paper beneath your hand. The dawn is rising again, pushing up towards the window. You stand slowly, ready to meet it.

He coughs, a rough sound that disturbs the quiet in your head, rustles the paper. 'However,' he continues, 'the Court recommends mercy for the prisoner, solely and only on account of her sex.'

You hear the words, but they are a jumble in your brain. Your hands move to find the edge of the table, your mind still in darkness.

'On account of my sex?' you whisper.

'Commuted to life in prison,' he says.

'On account of my sex?' you say again, feeling the cold creep of panic up your back. They are turning away, shuffling ready the next piece of paper.

'Did I not stand beside the men you've shot'—your voice scrapes across the silence, like a rusted gate—'dressed like them, armed like them…'

But they have already forgotten you, the door already closing behind them.

'…ready to die like them!' you shout.

You stand there a long time, not knowing what else to do, the dawn rising, breaking softly around you.

HIGHLY COMMENDED
Judith Wilson

About the Author

Judith Wilson is a London-based writer and journalist. She won 1st Prize for the London Short Story Prize 2019, 2nd Prize for the Colm Tóibín International Short Story Award 2016, and 3rd Prize for the Brick Lane Bookshop Short Story Award 2019. She was shortlisted for the Fish Short Story Prize 2022 and the Yeovil Literary Prize 2022. Her short stories have appeared in the Fairlight Book of Short Stories and prize anthologies. Many of Judith's short stories are inspired by a strong sense of place, particularly Liverpool, where she grew up. In her writing, she's drawn to exploring complex relationships and the lives of 'hidden women.'

Judith began writing fiction a decade ago. After completing the Faber Academy Writing a Novel course, she went on to do an MA in Creative Writing at Royal Holloway, University of London, graduating with Distinction in 2019. She originally studied English Literature at university, and for her MA at the University of Warwick her dissertation was on Rosamond Lehmann.

Alongside writing fiction, Judith has pursued a successful career in magazine journalism, focusing on interiors. Her articles have appeared in many magazines including *House & Garden*, *Homes & Gardens*, *The English Home*, *Living etc*, and *Country Homes & Interiors*. She is also the author of 14 books on interior design. Judith has lectured on Styling at the British Institute of Interior Design and the KLC School of Design.

Judith is currently writing a novel set in 19th-century Cornwall. When she's not in London, she goes to Cornwall, where she loves the wild seas, expansive vistas, and sense of history the region encapsulates. Judith is married to Anthony, and they have two grown-up children and a spaniel called Alfie. She can be found at www.judithwilsonwrites.com and on Instagram and X at @judithwrites.

BLACK CHRIST

By Judith Wilson

Black Christ is bleeding.

I stand below him and tilt my face, check again. His loins are red. Scarlet. Vermilion. A drop of blood flowers on my skin. It's his, then?

I smear my hand. No. It's mine.

I lick the blood away with a cautious tongue: metal-tart-taste. I wouldn't be surprised if it *was* his blood – Black Christ's – even though he's a twisted metal sculpture up there on the wall. Mam said: That sculptor, Arthur Dooley, he should burn in hell. Her words exactly.

One more lick. D mustn't see it or else –

What would he say, a nice girl like me? Covered in blood?

What he *said* was: See you under Black Christ, 2pm. You know the one?

Yes, I replied.

How could I not? It's been here a year, a Liverpool landmark since '69. And I've seen how the commuters - all fancy in their itchy office suits - crane their necks as they shoot on by, city princes in their Ford Cortina cars. Us kids, en route to school, we gather beneath the Christ sculpture, catcalling Jesus like he hears. Which he can't.

Obviously.

D isn't here yet.

I tilt my head again. The sculpture is a crucified man soaring 12 feet high in the air. Hello mate, I say, I'm glad we've time together. Black Christ projects like a rocket to the pigeon sky. He's fixed to the church: nails in his hands, knees, and bum. Dear Lord, that must have hurt. Mam said there were 1000 locals assembled, the day they unveiled him to the world.

It's a crying shame, she added, calling him 'The Resurrection of Christ'.

Under her breath, she muttered a Hail Mary, just in case.

Personally, I'm not a believer. Still -

It didn't take long for you – yes, you Jesus - to get nicknamed Black Christ on account of your wide, flat nose, and your sooty metal darkness. Yet I see that red tint, now I'm up close and personal, is paint, not blood.

And you're not exactly *black*, are you? Bronze, rather? The scarlet in your guts glitters as if you've been ripped apart with a pitchfork. I picture that sculptor wielding an oxyacetylene torch, in a warehouse on Scottie Road, like a devil in his paradise.

It looks like the pair of you had a fight. Did the artist wring your body into the correct shape, in pain, but soaring? Did it take days or weeks? You're the scandal of Toxteth, Black Christ, are you aware? Mam said so daily, after your – ahem, erection – as she liked to say.

D is ten minutes late.

That's if my Timex watch is working correctly. It was Mam's gift for my 13th birthday; it has a sky blue strap.

The wrapping paper was second-hand. I could see the marks from other peoples' Sellotape. But she said: Wear it for high days and holidays.

So, today is –

Not a holiday exactly. A high day, then? You tell me, Black Christ, with your arms diving in a perpendicular V. Except, you're heading Heaven-bound, aren't you?

Not deep-water-down, like me.

So, it's not a high day. Rather, a desperate hour. The truth is, I'm skiving off school. I should be playing hockey, with my pleated skirt fluttering in the Dingle wind, shouting: Me, Me, send it my way! If it was raining, which I'd prefer, we'd be on the gym bars.

I'd rather be anywhere but here.

D, where are you? By the way?

A new bubble of blood splutters on my arm. My cut is self-inflicted, do you see?

It's 2.15 pm and I hope no one clocks me. They won't guess I'm bunking off, as I've shoved my uniform away. I'm in Mam's cherry-print dress, so if someone was driving by, radio blaring, one hand rapping the driver's door, he won't think I'm a schoolgirl.

Right now, a leery man catcalls, forgets about Mungo Jerry and his Top 10 song.

I strike a pose, thumb my nose. Anyone would judge me a woman.

What d'you think of that, Black Christ?

And while I'm waiting, standing outside a church, even though it's Methodist, and I'm a lapsed Catholic and all, do you do any tricks?

Do you answer prayers? Are you *listening*?

I walk a few paces to catch an alternative view.

Mam says it's important to see the whites of a man's eyes when seeking the truth. It would be comforting if you were a woman, but statues are always men, right? Who would imagine Christ as a lady? Mam said you were modelled on a real man from Toxteth, with roots from the continents: Asia, Afro-Caribbean, Europe, Middle East, Native America. A melting pot of five out of the seven.

So, that leaves –

Well, I'm all for a joined up happy world, but Geography was never my strong point. I dropped it for Domestic Science and the days I carry home rice pudding and a lemon cake in my basket makes me happy, because Mam gets on a brew, and we don't go to bed hungry.

Tick tock, tick tock –

D – you *promised* you'd come.

I open my palms in supplication, Black Christ. It looks as if your arms are spread like a butterfly's wings, but your ribs are sticking out, and your legs are so skinny, tendons and muscles exposed. I may not be the smartest at school, but I know these physical terms. When Dad got injured by a falling car at the Ford Factory production line, he was four weeks in hospital. His leg was never the same, nor was his pay packet. Those bastards didn't want him back. Dad's right leg grew withered even as the left one rippled stronger to support his bulk.

One year, two, and then boom –

We only had a plywood coffin and no flowers. The eve of the funeral, when friends and neighbours visited to pay their respects and weep, candles flickering, he still had one fat leg and one thin. People said he was a good man and Mam cried buckets, but I couldn't.

Instead, I went out that night and I found D.

On the Toxteth scrubland, between this church and home, D linked my hand and fastened a daisy chain in my hair. He said: it's not your own colour, am I right, love? He was spot on. I'm black-haired (that's the Irish on Mam's side) but she favours the peroxide, so I'd borrowed her bottle of DIY bleach. The night I met D, I was 15, locks as golden as an angel. Before he laid me down in the pink willowherb, he said my cheeks were flushed like a sunset.

D made me his, all right.

He said he was 18. But there was a white circle on the fourth finger of his left hand.

He was kind until he wasn't, but then he left. And now –

I've been waiting an hour. This June heat, it's making me sick. Beneath my sandals, the pavement rises like a demon on the wing. I slide my back against the church's wall, so for one moment I can rest on my haunches. The skin grazes as I do so, and I ponder that pain has Holy beauty. I strike this pose often in the school loos, more frequently these last months. It's a good way to rest alone. Squatting on the toilet seat, no one can see your feet.

Sometimes, my mates yell out for me. Mostly I ignore them.

That slimy toilet paper is rubbish for wiping your eyes, let alone your bum.

D isn't coming, I feel it in my waters. I pace back to where I started. Hands on my hips, I squint at you, Black Christ, a little harder. D'you see me, mate?

Can you read my thoughts? Could you –

No, it's too much to ask.

But if I slid to my knees, would you pray with me?

Can you make things all right? Dear Lord?

This baby inside me resembles a piece of bacon, pink, and sizzling, like in Mam's breakfast pan. I've looked it up in my biology textbook. It's five-and-a-quarter inches long. *'At 18 weeks, the new mother feels a quickening.'* If I count back to Dad's funeral, that means –

I haven't told a soul. And I've tried all the tricks.

One night when Mam was church bound, I took the vodka beneath her bed.

Another time, I slid out her steel knitting needle and I –

She never understood why her baby blue sweater came unravelled.

That's why I need D to come. It was hard enough to reach him, in the telephone booth, which smelled of pee, twisting the phone cord and pushing in the pennies.

He said: See you under Black Christ, 2pm.

So, here I am.

But he's not coming is he, Black Christ? Your face looks as tattered as I feel. It's as if the iron tears you're crying have washed grooves in your cheeks, a thousand rivers for a thousand sins, one of which is mine. I imagine your tears splashing the pavement, but the dark circles are the ghosts of other people's gum. I lift a foot to check for dog poo.

I am clean.

I am clean.

But I'm not.

You're a dirty girl, get out! That's what Mam will say.

I'm on my knees now. When I rise there will be pockmarks, but they will fade. Not like the scars on my arms, in the crooks, pale rivers in the secret places no one sees.

A blade to skin takes my sorrows away.

As I'm here, Black Christ, don't you want this baby for your own? A tiny soul to keep you company. You must be so lonely up there, suspended between land and sky, caught in perpetual motion, yet forever frozen. If you do this one thing for me, I'll repay you, I promise. My hands make a steeple. *Please.* Take this growing alien away.

Because D isn't coming - is he?

I wait, I wait. Black Christ, I hope upon hope your love will invisibly swirl to fill me, as Mam insists it can, her head bent by the bed, her feet in furry slippers. And perhaps she's right. The longer I wait, the lighter I feel, like the puff of a dandelion, poised to fly.

I cross Princes Road, and right on cue, here's the bus to the terminal for the Mersey Ferry. I flag it down, and I swing on board. Are you with me, Black Christ? I believe you are, because here, someone's dropped a £1 note. It'll be just enough for the crossing to Birkenhead.

Ferry Cross the Mersey, as Gerry likes to sing, and I'll follow suit.

Black Christ, you're lighting the way, I believe it.

I board the ferry and I jostle the streams of passengers, the camel-coated commuters, the wide-mouthed mums with kids and the Beatles tourists from God-knows-where. There's the stink of salty chips and saltier air. Beneath my feet the boat thrums like an angry tiger, but I'm at peace now you're here. I scramble to the top deck and the wind catches my breath and slaps my hair. I hang over the side. It's a long way down to the milky chocolate of the waves below. Chop, chop, they go, splash-crash.

In the distance, the Welsh hills sparkle.

I think of your V-shaped soar to the Heavens, Black Christ. I picture the motion of your incessant upwards blast, even though you're nailed forever to that church. My foot is on the safety rail, and now, the other one joins it. I won't slip or fall because I'm a freeze-frame goddess. So what if someone shouts from behind? I don't care, I don't care.

I raise my arms, just like you. We're two of a kind, a mirror-image pair.

Are you watching, Black Christ? I trust in your goodness and your warmth.

Because here I go -

SHORTLISTED
Louise Morrish

About the Author
Louise is a librarian and author who lives with her family and canine writing buddy in Hampshire. She began writing fiction when she should have been studying for her Philosophy and Law degree at the University of Kent, many moons ago.

Louise has worked in all sorts of libraries in her thirty-year career, including public libraries, private collections, and both primary and secondary school libraries. She even once single-manned a tiny 18th-century haunted library. She currently manages a secondary school library in Hampshire and has the pleasure and privilege of enthusing teenagers to read.

Over the years, she has catalogued, shelved, recommended and championed tens of thousands of other people's books, whilst secretly nurturing an ambition to be published herself.

Her dream of seeing her own book on a shelf came true when her debut novel, *Operation Moonlight*, won the Penguin Random House First Novel competition in 2019. Her novel was published by Century in 2022, and she is now represented by literary agent LBA Books.

Louise is passionate about women's history. She

loves nothing more than discovering the stories of ordinary women in the past who achieved extraordinary things, but whom history has forgotten.

She is currently working on a new story, inspired by two female doctors who were medical pioneers in the First World War. When she isn't writing, Louise can usually be found running, albeit slowly, in the countryside.

THE ROARING GIRL

By Louise Morrish

At long last, you're here.

I've felt you in my bones for days, like the coming of a storm. Your arrival's stirred up the stagnant air in here, can you feel it?

Come, come, into my cell. Excuse the crunch of the floor; tis only a carpet of lice.

Closer still, into the candlelight. I wish to see you better, boy.

I won't bite.

You're not frightened of these blunted, rotting teeth, are you? They can't harm a worm.

Oh, I can see the question reflected in the black pools of your eyes. I know exactly what you're thinking: *How can a dead woman speak*?

You'd be forgiven for thinking me a corpse, boy. Wrapped in these rags, crawling with roaches. I've been brought low these past months. I wouldn't treat my dogs the way I've been treated in here. The beasts in the Bear Garden, baited though they be, live a better life than me.

Well, I'm not dead yet, boy.

Oh, you've brought quill and ink and paper. A proper little lawman, ain't you? Any food in that satchel of yours?

Bread, good. Cheese, good. A flagon of ale, a pipe. Did Lewknor tell you to bring all this? I bet he did. The toad.

Yes, leave it all there, by my feet.

Now, before we start, tell me my little girl is well.

What was that you said? I've had my ears boxed, and can only hear from one lobe.

You ask how I fare?

How do you think a condemned mother fares? Look at me, see the flesh on these arms, maggot-white. You'd be the same if they left you mouldering in the bowels of Newgate, boy. Caged like one of the beasts in the Bear Garden; like poor Old Harry Hunks perhaps. He was my favourite.

But unlike him, I refuse to be baited.

No need to explain yourself, young man, I know precisely why you're here. Lewknor sent you, didn't he? That rabid old cur I have the misfortune to call my husband. He wants answers, before it's too late. Before I hang.

He wants what's mine.

Well, he already has the only thing that matters to me.

Susannah.

He thinks Susannah is his...well, he never was the sharpest blade.

The bastard's cutting it fine, but then that's always his way.

You can run back to that filthy old sot, and tell him I'm not playing his games. I have other lovers, other means of buying the hangman off.

You thought Lewknor was my soul mate? He told you that, did he? Ha! Tis true, we've been together twenty years, but in that time we've each bedded many others. Whores and wastrels, both. And not only in the combination you're thinking.

Tomorrow, once I've paid off my old friend the hangman, I'll get my girl back. Gregory's never turned my coin away.

What was that? He's *dead*? You lie, boy! I've not heard word of that. Replaced by who? That clay-brained idiot? How do I know you aren't lying to me?

You give me your *word*? I'm expected to believe you?

Hand me that pipe, I need to smoke. To *think*.

This news changes all.

Did Lewknor know of this? I'll wager he did. Why else would you be here?

He bargains for my life then.

As I bargain for my daughter's.

My lips are sealed, til I see proof, certain proof, that my Susannah is safe and well, under Lewknor's roof.

She is both, you say?

How can I know you speak the truth?

Don't look at me like that. I could rip your throat out with these nails. Don't give me reason to place my hands around your delicate neck, press down upon that Adam's apple of yours, bobbing like a cork.

I've done it before, remember.

Oh, you're eyeing my manacles now are you, these rusted chains looped about my legs. Checking for the hundredth time they're secure. Don't think I didn't notice. I'm not blind.

Go on, reach into that satchel of yours. What have you brought as proof my daughter lives?

Give me that. To see such a precious keepsake in your hand makes me feel sick.

I would know my own child's locks anywhere. If you have brought me the hair of a horse, I will know it.

See this colour? Pure summer's gold. Brilliant as sunshine. My girl's golden tresses. She gets it from my side of the family, of course. Not his. Never his. All dark and troll-like on his side. My hair was once this blonde too, not that you can tell from these greasy hanks.

Do you know what torments me the most in here, boy? Not the lice, nor the roaches, not the cess-pit stink, nor the rough gaolers. Not the ever-darkness, not the time that stands still.

No, it's that my daughter, my darling Susannah, will have no memory of her mother.

Just as I have no memory of mine.

I vowed I wouldn't inflict the same fate on my Susannah. And yet, it seems fated to be. Unless we can come to some arrangement. I know why you're here. Lewknor wants me to spill my guts, reveal where I've hidden my cache, my horde. My only security against ruin.

He's sent you, thinking your sky-blue eyes and rosy lips will soften me.

Ha!

You have a troubled brow. I see the flicker of pulse in your neck bounding like a hare's. Don't fret, boy. I prefer my fruit ripened.

And in return for my secrets, what? You give me assurance that Susannah will be cared for? That no harm will come to her, after I'm gone.

A fair exchange, you say. But surely even you, green shoot that you are, can see Lewknor has all the power, he holds all the cards, at least while I'm locked up in here like some wild creature.

Yet that's not quite true. I have the only thing he craves.

I'll tell you my secret, in return for your promise.

Come closer. I'll softly whisper it in your ear, my voice a chill breeze upon your shivering cheek.

Quick, pay heed. Time is slipping away.

I'll tell you my secret, boy, but in return you must promise to take care of my girl. Do I have your word?

Pick up your quill then, young scribe. Dip your nib, if you'll pardon the expression. Write this down, word for word, for I won't repeat it. I'm about to reveal what Lewknor craves to know, if you listen carefully enough.

My story begins in the Barbican, four years after the defeat of the Armada. My father told me I came into the world with my fists doubled, a very tomboy and rump-scuttle from the first. He'd wanted a lad, of course, to take on his shoemaking business. And here I was, a useless girl. And yet, I never was a girl by inclination or manner. I enjoyed sporting with the boys my age, grew skilled at cudgel-play. By five, I could wrestle a lad twice my size to the ground without breaking a sweat.

All was well, until my mother died birthing my baby brother, who breathed his last as well. I was but six summers. The same age my Susannah is now. A disaster for a little girl, you might think. And it's true, I missed my ma with a pain akin to a vital organ ripped from my body.

But I was a sturdy wench, and my wound soon scarred over, my heart never quite the same again, but fixed well enough that no one noticed the absence.

Father did his best to raise me, but he had no chance, really. I was already my own captain.

The wimple and bodice made me itchy with unease, and I much preferred to dress in jerkin and britches. I soon became practised in sword-play and knife skills, and as a result my father despaired of me ever finding my feminine side.

If an accident of birth had not encumbered me with breasts and a cunny, I would have sought glory in the wars, or sailed across the oceans, seeking my fortune. But it wasn't to be.

Or so I thought.

While other girls were content to embroider samplers, or powder their faces, I much preferred to spend my free time at the Bear Garden. From the moment I stepped into that blood-soaked place, seething with foreign ambassadors and spies, I was beguiled.

At night, the place was so dark, bounded by trees, that a girl needed cats' eyes to see. I had such eyes.

The sport of baiting bears, bulls, even horses sometimes, enthralled me. The way the bears roared, and the bulls tossed the dogs in the air, then caught them on their horns again. Once, I saw a pony with an ape lashed to its back, and the dogs were set loose, and the horse and ape did scream so to make the ears bleed.

On one or two occasions, a solitary lion was baited. A more regal creature I never did see. But even the lions were no match for the dogs, in the end.

I grew to love the dancing in that place, and the music and the fireworks. Once, some enterprising soul fixed a rose of gunpowder to the roof, and set it on fire, showering apples and pears down upon the crowd. People scrambled to gather the bruised and charred fruit, as rockets fell from the sky. It caused a great fright!

But I've gone down a snickleway.

Are you still writing this down? Good. Give me a swig of that ale, boy, while we're at it.

Ah, that wets the whistle.

Sup with me?

Suit yourself, then.

So, it was here in the Bear Garden, at the age of nine or maybe ten, I fell in with a gang of thieves. They taught me the art, and it is an art, of the cutpurse. I slipped between the legs of the crowd, like a slippery little eel through weed, and grew swift with a pair of scissors, let me tell you. But pickpocketing soon became my favourite sport, and I got good at it. I started at the bottom, as a 'rub', the last link in the chain. The 'file' (the leader, to you) did the picking of the pockets, while his mate (the 'bull') jostled the victim and caused a distraction. And then the loot was quickly passed to me, the smallest, nimblest member of the gang, and off I would scurry, away through the crowd, with shouts of 'Stop that boy! Stop thief!' ringing in my ears.

I never got caught.

As I grew into adulthood, so too did my reputation as someone to trust. Soon, the most notorious thieves and rascals were gracing my door. Men like Mull Sack, who once, it is claimed, emptied Buckingham's heavy pockets; and Crowder, who liked to dress as a bishop and hold up a stagecoach with pious force.

For these men, and many others, I was soon fencing stolen goods, and buying the hangman off with ill-gotten loot. By the time I came of age, I'd given up the pickpocketing lark, and instead made my living selling filched trinkets back to those stupid fools who'd lost them in the first place.

Your quill's dry again?

Dip it then, boy!

What do you mean, you don't understand? It's quite simple. Let's say, for argument's sake, a citizen was robbed on the highway. Well, if he came to Moll soon after, his precious things would likely be returned to him, minus my cut of course.

My house in Fleet Street became a refuge, as well as a repository of lost property. A sanctuary for those rogues who sought my protection. Over time, my subtle influence in Newgate made me more powerful than a whole bench of the most righteous judges. I supped with Gregory the hangman, knew each turnkey by name, and did business with Ralph Briscoe, clerk of Newgate, the prettiest fellow I ever did set my eye upon.

Don't give me that look, young man. Have you never coveted a forbidden fruit?

Ralph picked juries for me, sought reprieves for my men, and was faithful to the end. In return, I would bait a bull with the fiercest of my dogs for him. We made a formidable partnership, Ralph and I.

Over the next few years, my world steadily expanded, to take in most of London. Once, early on, I was nabbed by a guard, who'd been startled by my male attire. For I had begun by then to wear britches and doublet as my daily costume, and also smoke a pipe. But though the guard locked me in a cell that night, a word on the sly with the Lord Mayor, a man who enjoyed a good bear baiting, soon saw me walk free.

My second encounter with the manacles of justice came some months later, and required rather more cunning to slip free of. This is what happened: two of my agents had relieved a farmer of his silver pocket watch, during a tavern brawl. The next day, the victim made his way to my door, sensible fellow that he was. Of course, I promised to recover the said watch, for a tidy sum of course, just as soon as I reprimanded the miscreants responsible for such a terrible act.

Yes, I'm a kind and merciful soul, boy, though I resemble some beggar you might piss on in the street.

But I'd made a grave error. As I sent the farmer on his merry way, what do you think he spied nestled amongst the swag glittering in my window? Only his damned pocket watch, swinging by its silver chain.

Give that farmer his due, he didn't raise a fuss there and then. He bid me farewell, and it wasn't til later that a guard called by, and I found myself in gaol once more. But all was not lost. The guard had taken the farmer's watch into safe keeping, to be presented at my trial as evidence of my guilt. But when asked to produce the timepiece in court, well could that watch be found? Not anywhere! Oh dear, oh dear. Where *could* it have got to?

I hope you're getting all this down, young man. Your quill has stopped its jerky scratchings again, I see.

Well, after that I was a careful girl. Living within the shadow of Newgate, and knowing the prison yard as well as the Globe Tavern, I made sure that suspicion never fell on me again. I walked a hidden path, sheltered by that familiar band of thieves I'd grown up amongst. Like family to me, they were.

I expect you know well what they said of me, don't you, boy? 'By accident a woman, by habit a man.'

But I saw myself as neither man nor woman, but both. I wore a petticoat under my doublet, and both served me well. I had a woman's guile, and a man's grit.

Unlike most men, though, I condemned violence in my crew; there was enough bloodshed in the Bear Garden.

My one true friend from the first was a fellow by the name of Banks. He was a vintner of Cheapside, and I met him after he'd fallen foul of a rival gang, and sought my help. One day, bored and befuddled by his own drink, he devised a wager. He bet me £20 I wouldn't ride from Charing Cross to Shoreditch, by horse no less, dressed entirely as a man in britches and doublet and boots and spurs.

Well, I took him up on the wager, of course. And even added my own flourish, with trumpet and banner. And the eyes of all London were upon me, as I rode. I reached Bishopsgate with no one any the wiser as to my true gender. But there, an orange-wench I once wooed recognised me, and shouted out 'Moll Cutpurse! Moll Cutpurse!' And a noisy crowd did mob me then. Many laughed, but some, including a number of fearsome women, were keen to tear me from the saddle and divest me of my offending garments.

I was rescued by a wedding ceremony up ahead, which distracted the baying women and grabby men for long enough that I was able to spur my horse and gallop away. I made it to Shoreditch at last, and lightened my friend's pockets by £20.

That's not the end of the story. I'd caused a public scandal, and that very day I was hauled before the Court to answer a charge of 'appearing publicly in mannish attire.' I was sentenced to do penance dressed in nothing but a white sheet at Paul's Cross, during the following Sunday morning service. I made sure I had three quarts of sack the night before, and swaggered there in good humour, to stand in the rain, the sheet wrapped tight like a shroud. Many of the congregation cheered to see me, and as I was set free at last I was accosted by some saucy folk, begging me to reveal myself in full.

It was later that day, dressed again in doublet and jerkin, that this story takes a dark turn. Back at my beloved Bear Garden, I was met with the worst of news.

Old Harry Hunks, the favourite of my bears, had fought his final battle. His death was like a blow to my heart. I'd cared for the animal since a cub, fed him morsels of fruit, roared with him in victory when he loped from the ring, injured and bleeding, but alive. They called me the Roaring Girl, for the strength of my love for that bear.

The big old beast was free of chains now, free to roam the forests of his birth again, if only in spirit.

But my heart was sore.

At least I still had my cherished dogs. My two bull mastiffs, Raleigh and Drake, were my heart and soul, and I cared for them like the children I didn't yet have. They each had a trundle-bed by the fire, with sheets and blankets, and were fed the choicest cuts of meat.

And then, fate dealt me another blow.

Lewknor, that useless drunkard who sent you here, crashed into my world.

He had the swagger, the wink, a lewd suck on his pipe.

Thought he was God's gift.

And I, brought low by Old Harry's death, thought he was too. At first.

Lewknor knew how much I wanted to keep that old bear. He suggested we have the beast stuffed. He'd heard tell of some Italians, who'd taken the skull and leg bones of a horse and mounted the animal's frame on a wooden armature. The skin they preserved with some sort of wax, then packed the body with wool.

You snare me with that look again, boy, as though I am the Devil taken female form. Your throat is stuffed with fear, I know, but hear me out.

Lewknor tracked down a man in Limehouse who claimed to be able to do the same for my Harry. And so it came to be that the beast was immortalized. I now shared my home with a hairy guardian standing seven feet tall, sharp-clawed and yellow-toothed.

It was a sight to greet you in the morning, let me tell you.

Of course, Lewknor does nothing for nothing. He wanted payment from me. He wanted all that was mine.

So he took it all. And then some.

No sooner had we wed, than he was forcing himself on me. Day and night, unremitting. Brutal and merciless. When he could get it up.

Being young, I fell pregnant quickly.

With no mother to teach me the ways of birthing, it

was a wonder we both survived. Susannah was born
sheathed in her caul, like a mermaid's purse.

She'll never drown.

Lewknor, he drowned himself in ale every night,
and left me all alone. Useless waste of skin.

If he was a privy stool, I wouldn't shit on him. You
can tell him that.

With a child to feed now, I worked harder than ever,
yet Lewknor drank away everything we earned.

What would you have done, boy?

I had to protect my Susannah.

But where to hide my coins, my loot, where
Lewknor couldn't steal it?

The answer came to me that violent night. After our
last, most terrible fight, as Lewknor lay bleeding and
bawling on our bedroom floor, I crawled away with my
knife, and woke Susannah from her slumber.

Swiftly, I hid our only hope in plain sight, and swore
my daughter to secrecy. Told her our treasure must be
guarded.

She's kept her promise.

And now I've told you.

Were you listening?

Will you keep your word?

I hope so, for your sake.

SHORTLISTED
Josie Turner

About the Author

Josie Turner lives in Kent and has worked in the NHS for over twenty years. She has had prose and poetry published in a range of journals including Brittle Star, The North, Mslexia, The Interpreter's House, Roanoke Review, Gordon Square Review, Scoundrel Time and The Four-Faced Liar. She has won the Brighton Prize and the Welsh Poetry Competition and received the Sue Lile Inman Award for Fiction from the Emrys Foundation. In 2023 she placed second in the Elmbridge Literary Competition. Josie can be found on X @JosieTurner20.

WELL WATER

By Josie Turner

Amelia had a hankering to take everything inside – chickens in wintertime, dogs grown too old to work, the tenderest seedlings she secretly warmed by the stove. When she married Thomas she took in his baby son Charley, jogging him happily on her hip and swiping away a hard chubby hand whenever he brought it down against her jaw, or twisted the fabric of her collar. She'd rescued Tom as a thirty-year-old widower when she herself had been only sixteen – or he'd rescued her. One or the other. The town held Amelia to be the lucky one when she married a farmer and escaped the society of many sisters.

Baby Charley had almost gone to an orphanage – Amelia put a stop to that. His mother had been dead for five months when Amelia arrived at the farmstead and found her new stepson sitting up in an iron pan, like a kid captured by a wicked witch in a fairytale.

'Hey Charley,' she said, swinging him up to kiss his dirt-crusted cheek. 'I'm your Momma now.'

And she ached to take in Charley again when he got shot, at only eighteen – but he was across state lines, and the doctor forbade him to travel. So Tom went out to him and Charley died in his arms, rising and falling like a flame, while Amelia sat in the kitchen with her head in her lap, her fingertips rubbing together as though she could feel her boy's coarse straw hair between them.

God did not bless them with children of their own. But He provided Amelia with plenty of things to take in: wounded farmhands, stricken animals and plants, and another needy baby, Charley's baby – unmistakably his own baby, with the very same astonished cobalt eyes and halo of blond hair – who Tom conveyed back to the farm along with Charley's unexpected widow, Elisabeth.

*

'All Tom's family are light-complexioned,' said Amelia one day, chopping vegetables at the table while Elisabeth nursed baby Chad. 'This 'un gets his yallowy looks from Tom's people. Also from you.'

Elisabeth had long fine hair that didn't amount to much. Amelia could see a pink scalp shining when the girl looked down to croon to her baby.

'Want me to hold him for a spell?' she asked, when she'd put the knife in the sink and wiped the peelings into a bowl for the pigs.

'Go on,' said Elisabeth, hoisting the fat kid over the corner of the table. She was a knacky mother but never wanted to hold him for long. She didn't have many places to put him, aside from her slight bosom. Amelia was stout and ambidextrous: she could tuck a child in her apron or sling him on her back while she ran a broom around the kitchen floor. Chad would snuffle for his new grandma, sleep for her, bare his smattering of teeth for her, while Elisabeth slipped out of the house to find a quiet spot of shade by the pond or behind the barn.

*

'Poor kid,' Amelia said to Tom, when they blew out their candle at night.

'Which one?'

'Both. Nothing in it. She don't look old enough to chew her food.'

He turned over, facing the square of fabric Amelia had hung at the bedroom window.

'She's old enough.'

*

Amelia was part of the house, and it was part of her. She could see every room with her eyes shut, and feel the old walls breathing. There were dents in the floor where Charley had played rough, and scars in the doorframe where they'd measured his growth. He'd got to be a tall man. She could hear Elisabeth brushing her hair, drawing the long paddle along the underside of its pale rippling expanse. When Chad opened his mouth to cry Amelia was by his side before he made a sound.

'Gamma's here, baby,' she whispered, lifting him free of his damp napkin.

Amelia never felt the ghost of Tom's first wife. There were no images of her anywhere, but she'd been a fine-looking woman who begat a fine-looking son and grandson. Amelia loved those boys on her behalf, and so the dead woman was content to lie quietly, like the chill water in the aquifer underneath the land.

I'd've liked a daughter, Amelia thought shyly, looking at Elisabeth while the girl washed a bowl of berries. She had strong brown fingers and good-shaped arms. She'll marry soon, thought Amelia, and then we won't see Chad no more. Farmers' sons all around the county wanted to pay their addresses to the girl.

Tom sat the boy on his knee in the evenings. He'd whittled his grandson a toy horse.

The house was full of a strange buzzing vitality which Amelia attributed to the child, growing like a green shoot in a field. She stood him against the doorframe and measured him against his father, cutting a notch in the soft wood.

*

When Amelia saw them both together she was standing at the top of the staircase, looking down around its newel post into the kitchen. Tom had a broad hand splayed on Elisabeth's back. Their faces were together, and for a moment Amelia though the girl was sick, or swooning, or whispering something to her father-in-law. But they stood so still, for so long, and made no sound until a voluptuous kiss broke between them. Amelia knew somehow that it wasn't the first kiss – it wasn't a moment of revelation for them, but one of confirmation. A handshake between conspirators. She got all that from the shape of his hand, the flex of her shoulders. A pot of beans bubbled on the stove. Outside, the wind rustled unripe crops.

Chad was napping in a dresser drawer Amelia had layered with old torn petticoats. She turned and went to kneel beside him, stroking the velvet of his cheek, thinking Charley, oh my Charley.

*

Amelia guessed she didn't have long. She'd forgotten her age. She didn't own a mirror but she saw herself in reflective surfaces – shirred in the pond, bulbous on the side of the one good pot. In her mind's eye she saw her mother's face, pinched with care. Her hands were rough and red.

Tom's hands had been so familiar. Her mother said a good marriage was a pair of hands – separate but connected, put together in prayer. She yearned to feel again the rope of her husband's spine, with her face cupped against his shoulder, but she was an old woman now and not for embracing. She remembered how he'd shot the horse with the broken leg – cleanly, kindly, with the pragmatic competence he brought to everything he did. 'Good old girl,' he'd said to the beast, patting her white-striped muzzle for the last time. 'You know, don't you?'

Well I'm not some damned old hoss, thought Amelia, peeling the ten thousandth potato of her life, not even noticing where the blunt knife sawed at her fingers.

*

Tom was getting a ride into the city. Their neighbour Clemence appeared along the track, his trap jinking in the distance as he halloo'd towards the farmstead. He'd offered to take Tom to the bank. They all stood on the porch to watch his approach – Tom in his church suit, Elisabeth in a new blue poplin dress Amelia had run up for her, Amelia herself in overalls and standing back a little. She could see Tom and Elisabeth in silhouette, their shoulders almost touching.

She'd settled Chad upstairs, among the petticoats, after Elisabeth had given him a quick kiss – the girl was hectic today, had needed her dress buttoned with the ebony hook while she held up her hair and Amelia worked behind her like a lady's maid.

Maybe that's the plan, Amelia had thought, as the buttons slipped home: maybe they'll keep me on as a maid.

'Mornin'!' called Clemence, tipping his hat. 'Ye're a sight for sore eyes!' He kept a large slow son at home, who had an eye for Elisabeth.

'Never mind your sweet talk,' said Tom, clasping his overnight bag. He turned to kiss his women goodbye. Amelia inhaled the old smell of tobacco and linden water. Everything about him was the same, but changed, as though the man in the moon had beamed down to take his place. She saw Elisabeth on tip-toe, whispering something in his ear. The hem of the blue dress rose from her slippers, the hem Amelia had spent hours stitching.

Tom swung himself up into the trap next to their old friend, and with much waving and teasing and last-minute panics, after the horse had taken a long drink at the trough, and beneath the constant fine rain of Clemence's geniality, the two men set off down the long shady track that led to the road. Amelia put an arm around Elisabeth's shoulder, but with the other hand she fingered the bowl of peelings secreted in one of her pockets. Elisabeth stood waving to the men, calling farewells, rocking her body from side to side. Beneath the hilarity Amelia could hear chickens scratching in their pen, crops rising in the fields, the blond lashes growing on Chad's eyelids. Amelia thought of him with a great surge of love – the boy she'd taken in.

Once the men had dwindled to nothing, Amelia took her arm from Elisabeth's shoulder, drew the old kitchen knife from her overall pocket and reached up and around until the sharpened blade found the girl's windpipe. It was easy to do. Elisabeth stiffened and struggled as she fell backwards but there was no sound apart from a rasping, and then the liquid sounds of her blood. There was a lot of blood, as Amelia knew there would be. The porch was strewn with straw.

Upstairs, Chad gave a cry.

'In a moment,' called Amelia to him.

She tried to fold up the body, to catch the blood, but it was hopeless. Lithe Elisabeth gained weight as she died, so it was easiest to drag her off the porch by the heels, her loose head bopping on each step. The pig pen was far away and Amelia felt perspiration dripping into her eyes as her arms seemed to sag from their sockets, but she was a strong woman and soon the body was huddled against the fence. It took great effort to force the wet, slippery mass up and over – Elisabeth teetered before tumbling into the pen. The pigs stood frozen for a moment, and then they reacted.

During the feeding, Amelia brought the bowl of potato peelings from her overall and dropped it by the fence, just beyond the pigs' reach. It was like a painting, she thought – a young girl doing her chores, overbalancing on the fence and falling in. No-one knew the pigs hadn't been fed for two days, while Amelia had saved up kitchen scraps.

She stood for a moment – just a moment – to

watch the girl disappearing.

It was her or me, she shrugged.

Back at the farmstead, Chad was hollering.

'Coming, my sweet,' called Amelia, as she took off her overall and washed her body at the pump, knowing it wasn't the farmhands' day and she could walk around the property in her birthday suit if she chose. Then she took the bundle back indoors, collecting the bloody knife where it lay on the porch. There was a lot of mess to clear up – really, a very great lot – but she had plenty of time. Her overall would go in the furnace. The knife could be washed in the sink. It would take buckets and buckets of well-water to clean the porch and the bloody trail leading to and from the pig pen, but she had all day. All day and every day.

Chad would grow stronger and taller, rising alongside the memory of his father. Underneath their feet the deep aquifer would continue to nurture them all, she told herself, year after year, constant and unseen.

SHORTLISTED
Cheryl Burman

About the Author
Originally from Australia, Cheryl Burman now lives in the Forest of Dean, UK, and, like Tolkien, Rowling and many others, the Forest inspired her to write. She started with middle grade fantasy, discovered a taste for historical fiction, and has more recently moved on to historical fantasy, which she rather likes. Given she is lucky enough to live in a place chock-a-block full of history, legend and myth, there is much to draw on, like the story which appears in this anthology.

Two of her novels have won awards, as have several of her flash fiction pieces. Some of these are included in her collection, *Dragon Gift*, while others are published in various anthologies.

A keen student of writing craft, Cheryl has had articles published on writing-related topics both online and in print and maintains a popular writing tips post on her blog.

As Cheryl Mayo, she is the chair of Dean Writers Circle and a founder of Dean Scribblers, which encourages creative writing among young people in her community.

Find her at https://cherylburman.com/

Follow her on twitter @cr_burman or on Facebook @CherylBurmanAuthor.

WHO CAN BELIEVE IN WITCHES IN THE YEAR OF OUR LORD, 1906

By Cheryl Burman

'You know how they found her?'

Sergeant Cooper is smug above his thick, dark moustache. Ellen doesn't know, only that however they found her, it will bode her, Ellen, no good. She gazes out the parlour window to the rows of herb pots blossoming in the May warmth and the tidy beds where flowers will soon spill their health-giving profusion.

'Wandering through the trees, she was.' Cooper leans towards Ellen, his voice a heavy buzz in her ear. 'Three days and nights she been in there, lost.'

Ellen faces him, her expression neutral. Cooper is not the first fool she has suffered.

'Hair tangled with leaves and grass, skirts torn.' He leers. 'Could see her bloomers, filthy as they was.'

'Poor soul,' Ellen murmurs.

'Ha! You might say so, given she was waving a hazel stick, calling out about keeping the *witches* away.' His button black eyes corrode only the back of Ellen's head, for she has returned to her inspection of the garden.

Yes, this is what he has come for. Markey has been loud in his accusations of witchcraft. *Who has my stolen money?* he demanded. A simple enough question for such as Ellen. She bade him peer into a crystal, the man tells all who will listen (there are many), revealing therein secrets he would not have learned, scandalous secrets. Afterwards, a madness not of this world struck down his daughter, his granddaughter. They languish in the asylum. Now his wife will join them.

Ellen keeps her gaze neutral. She will not help Cooper with denials or statements of innocence. He can torture it from her, as they have ever done with those accused. Cooper, with his judgemental morality, would have fitted well with the past. Ellen envisions him in a coned witchfinder's hat, cloak flying behind like crow's wings as he leads the excited procession to the dunking pond, or the hanging tree. She shuts the images away. There will be no dunking, no hanging. There will be shame, humiliation, and the death of a hard-earned livelihood.

Sensing trouble – or scandal, depending on their natures – neighbours have gathered. They shuffle their feet on the cracked paved path from the front door to the iron gate, and beyond onto the dirt road. They whisper, point, scowl.

'All your doing, *Mother* Hayward,' Cooper jeers. 'Which is why you're coming with me, charged all proper.' He unfolds a piece of paper and reads aloud, with particular enjoyment of certain words: 'unlawfully', 'pretended witchcraft', 'deceive'.

Ellen lifts her chin, asks, 'Who will feed my hens?'

'They'll be fed.' The policeman uses his dusty boot to push a white bird across the bare floor boards. It cackles, lifts its wings in protest. 'Or become food.' He smirks.

Ellen turns from his smugness, seeking a sympathetic

eye among the crowd which has now seeped into the parlour itself. Granny Kear gives a slight nod and the hens are off the list of Ellen's worries. Outside, the flowers and massed pots will survive the season's gentle, damp warmth. She need not concern herself over hens and plants. Much else remains.

She squints at the policeman through eyes grown weak with age and too much close work. 'I'm no witch, Sergeant Cooper,' she says. 'Who can believe in witches in the year of our Lord, 1906?'

Cooper snorts. 'We'll let the magistrate decide that. And don't you be taking our Lord's name in vain, else it'll go worse for you.' He grips her elbow. 'Get your coat.'

The neighbours shuffle awkwardly in the constraints of the hallway. Room is made for Ellen and her uniformed escort.

Cooper is forced to stop when Granny Kear steps forward, presses Ellen's shoulder with arthritically knobbled fingers. 'Don't thee fret, Ellen, it'll come out all right.'

'More witches, a whole coven likely,' Cooper mumbles.

Granny Kear ignores his glare and steps aside.

*

The cold of the cell's flagstones leaches through Ellen's thin soles. She wraps her shawl about her shoulders and sits on the cot. There is one blanket, no pillow, but Ellen has never rested her head on a pillow, a luxury for better-off folk than she's ever been. The evening darkens through the high, barred window. This place where they hold her is not far from her old haunt, the workhouse. Not that any here will learn that from her. Twenty-five years ago. Busy with the townsfolk's ailments and life's everyday problems, Ellen's chances for reflection are few, though greater in number than the times she wishes to reflect. Now her mind insists, because if Granny Kear is wrong, the workhouse is where Ellen will end her days. The straw mattress crackles beneath the sudden trembling of her slim weight.

'Hey, you, are you the witch?'

The question is tossed across the gap between the rows of cells. Ellen ignores it.

'Cast a spell on 'em all, sent 'em mad!'

Shocked intakes of breaths, broken by giggles.

'They burn witches, don't they?' Laughter.

'Where's the cat?' Shrieked amusement.

Others take up the calls, their heckling merging into one strident screech to assail Ellen's ears. Her pulse thumps. A thug in uniform paces down the barely lit passageway, battering a truncheon against bars – and fingers clenched to the bars, if too slow to be removed – boosting the din with his shouts of shut up you poxy whores.

Ellen remains on the cot, her hands in their half-mittens clenched beneath her bony buttocks.

Whore.

The word rattles in her tired, frightened brain.

It's the same word hissed many years ago in Ellen's face by her sour-faced sister-in-law. Her brother stood by, arms dangling, useless when not at his fishing.

Whore.

Ellen is back in the tiny room with its bed as narrow as the gaol cot, a scratched chest for her clothes the only other furniture. Her sister-in-law spat out her righteousness.

'We took you in, gave you a home, let you make a respectable living. Look how you repay us.'

The baby, pinkly new, squalled his hunger.

The gaol heckles fall away, the prisoners retreat into the dark places of their cells. There are whispers, cackles – forced or otherwise. Minutes pass. The air chills. An hour, perhaps. Snores, coughs, snuffles assault the silence. They are feeble, ineffectual against Ellen's spinning mind.

She shifts on the mattress, lies on her side to face the stone wall, and eases her stiff legs onto the cot. She keeps her boots on. Her heart beats with emotions she didn't know she still possessed. They don't belong with the calm, respectable, widowed Mrs Ellen Hayward, sought after wise woman and herbalist.

For over twenty years, people have trotted out their petty problems, laid them before her to deal with. Rashes, persistent headaches, a child with a wheezing cough. A lover gone astray or not yet caught. A lost brooch, mislaid money. Or was it stolen? Ellen advises, offers herbs and potions of her own learned and tried concoctions. Old people, mothers, those with the bloom of youth on their cheeks, show their gratitude with plant cuttings, a flitch of bacon, a collar of lace. A hen or two. So much time has passed. She has dragged herself to respectability. Wide awake, Ellen's mind insists on diving into its well of ancient, stifled memories.

Orphaned, plain, sullen, a resented burden on her brother's family, which only her skilful dressmaking diminished, barely. Until he came, the well-dressed customer with his smooth words and smoother promises. *Come walk with me by the river*, he said, taking her arm and leading her to the clifftop paths where his caresses and summer's breezes gently fanned Ellen's ardour.

My sweet Ellen. He stroked her arms, her neck, pulled her close, drew her down into the green shade of the high bracken where lovers have hidden for centuries. She gave herself, grateful to be desired.

We will marry.

His last words to her, before he left the village with the stealth, and doubtless the complacency, of a satiated tomcat.

Cloaks are a wondrous device for hiding the consequence of illicit love, but no cloak can hide a shameful birth. So there she was, in the bedroom with the wooden chest and an apoplectic sister-in-law, exposed in all senses.

Cast out by her brother and his wife, Ellen walked with head down to the river ferry, her newborn son cradled against her in his makeshift sling. The villagers traced her banishment with condemning gazes. A cloth bag was slung over her shoulder. All for the baby, her own meagre belongings sacrificed to the ease of cheap travel. Those sharing the ferry with her kept their distance, in case her sin should taint them. They huddled at one end like puppies in a box, wishing the cold journey to be over, their minds on warming fires and hot food.

As on the homeward side of the broad river, Ellen had nowhere to lay her and the baby's heads. She wandered up the steep road, past windows where chinks of candlelight gleamed through drawn curtains. The scent of roasting meats tickled her nostrils. She found shelter in the porch of the great church, and the next day used her few pennies to rent a hovel of a cottage.

She squirms on the gaol cot, crackling the straw, and shudders a breath. Tears not shed for decades prick her eyes. The cottage, more ruin than building. A broken table, a glassless window hung with a hessian sack. A freezing wind gusted through the gap under the door to dampen the already weak warmth of the fire. The baby weakened too. When the men came, they found his cheeks sunken and his cries thin.

*

It's near dawn when sleep captures Ellen, briefly, before banging on the bars shocks her awake. Gruel for breakfast, eaten in silence at a long table with other inmates. They return to their cells.

Ellen has a visitor.

'How long must I be here?' she asks Sergeant Cooper.

'As long as it takes.'

He stands outside her cell, suggesting his visit will be brief. Ellen stays seated on the cot. She wants to ask about the hens, except it would give him pleasure to taunt her. Instead she says, 'How is Mrs Markey?'

Cooper's button eyes gleam. He twists the end of his

moustache. 'Not only her what gone mad.'

She will not ask about this either, despite the faster pattering of her heart. Cooper will tell her, he can't help himself.

'The son, George. Neighbour found him in his kitchen, rambling nonsense, neighbour says, about *witchery* being practiced on his family.' He pokes a dirty-nailed finger through the bars, waggles it. 'I wonder who he be thinking of?'

Ellen folds her hands in her lap to hide their trembling.

Some days ago, Markey came to her house, hat scrunched in his black-nailed fingers, garbling a tale of money, a substantial amount, stolen from his home, from a locked drawer in a locked room.

'Who stole it, Mother Hayward? Find 'em, tell me.' He paced among the hens, muttering about not trusting anyone, not even family.

Cooper's cough interrupts Ellen's thoughts. 'Your old friend Doctor Carlton, it was him sent George to the asylum.' He squints at her, the knowing curve of his full lips peering through the shrubbery of his moustache.

When Ellen keeps her silence, Cooper humphs and turns to leave. 'No silences in court, *Mother* Hayward. We'll hear it all then.' He bows, mocking her, and strides away. His boots clump on the stone flags.

Doctor Carlton. Ellen pulls in her lips, seeing it all again, plain as day.

The doctor strode into the chilly hovel, no polite knocking. He glanced at the squalling baby, frowned at the freezing, filthy room, and shook his head. He looked questioningly at his companion. 'Workhouse,' the other said. Well fed, this one, with plump red cheeks sprouting a wiry ginger beard.

'No.' Ellen hugged her son closer, as if the mere feel of her breasts might nourish him. 'No, please.'

'You want the babe to die of hunger, exposure?' The doctor peered into the scrunched face.

'We could take the babe, leave you,' the ginger man said. 'Easy enough to find a home for it, once it's been fattened up.' When he poked the baby's chest, Ellen gagged at his sour breath.

'What's it to be?' Doctor Carlton said. His tone was almost kindly.

*

There's a new prisoner for the inmates to gloat over. A skeletal lass, caught for thieving a ribbon. She huddles in a corner, crying. The women either comfort or curse her, depending on their tolerance for noisy fright. For now, they ignore Ellen. There will be ample opportunity to return to her after her trial, if she is convicted.

The workhouse inmates didn't ignore her arrival, the baby adding to the drama. They clustered around, glad of a fresh tale, especially one spiced with immorality. Whispers tracked Ellen's movements by day and hung in the long dormitory's fuggy air at night. Lying on the iron cot with her son folded against her, she closed her ears to salacious gossip.

Watery, lukewarm gruel kept her from starvation, but the baby did not thrive. He refused her derisory offerings and lifted his own curled fist to chew. His eyes were screwed tight, his too-thin face wrinkled like an un-ironed shirt.

'If'n he won't feed, they'll sell him to the baby far-mer.' The words were hissed into Ellen's ear from the next bed, less than two handspans away.

An ancient woman with face and throat made of the same stuff as her rumpled brown dress, this one had held back from the accusing glares.

'Baby farmer?' Terror seethed in Ellen's gut. 'No.'

A dry, cackling laugh. 'It's a way to be relieved of the object of your shame, girl. Start over.' The old woman snorted. 'And mebbe the babe will find himself loving parents.'

Ellen shakes in horror. More like he will end as a tiny corpse in a rough-made grave beside a stinking privy.

'No.'

The word soughed across the space and the old woman caught it, returned it with a muttered, 'There be a second way.'

*

Dust motes lit by early morning sunlight through the high window float in the corner of Ellen's cell. She blinks, hauls her stiff bones to a sitting position and eases her legs to the floor. The chill of the flags pierces her stockinged feet, snakes its way up her body to nestle in the pit of her stomach.

Today is the day the magistrate will make his decisi-on.

She forces down breakfast's gruel, gagging. Back in her cell, she asks for water, a cloth and a comb, and is handed them with a shrug. She washes her face, brushes her black skirt with the damp cloth, twists her grey, thin hair into as neat a bun as she can with no benefit of a mirror. She sits on the straw mattress, hands in her lap, and waits.

Like she waited for the crone from the workhouse to whisper what this second way might be. Curled on her side, the woman had reached under her mattress and pulled out a stained calico pouch, bulging with whatever it held.

'Take it,' she hissed. 'I've no more need of it.'

Ellen drew back. 'What is it?'

The turnkey raps the bars of Ellen's cell with his truncheon.

'Time,' he says.

He unlocks the door, beckoning her out. She walks stiff-necked into the passageway, eyes on the man's black-coated back.

Heckling and laughter shadow her short journey to the outer door.

'See you back here soon!'

'Cast spells on 'em all.'

'Fly away.'

There'll be no flying away. Not this time.

*

'Ellen Hayward.'

Ellen startles at her name spoken in the clarion tones of the court clerk. The words of the charges reach her like the distant rumble of thunder over the river. Threatening, impersonal.

'… she did unlawfully use certain craft or means or device, to wit, by pretended witchcraft …'

She stares ahead as the first witness, Sergeant Cooper, is called, aware that every seat and bench in the high-ceilinged room is crammed to bursting with spectators. Aware too of Cooper's pompous accusations destroying, word by malicious word, the life she has carefully, assiduously created. Her chest tightens. She clutches the railing of the dock to save herself from falling.

There would be a judgement, a reckoning, one day. Ellen has always understood this. Yet over the years the understanding faded like curtains at a too sunny window, until only the barest pattern remains.

The memory of the workhouse plays more clearly in her head than the courthouse scene.

The crone had eased herself half upright, her bony shoulders in their greying nightgown pushed against the iron bedstead. She loosened the drawstring of the pouch, pulled it open and thrust it towards Ellen. The escaping scent writhed in the air, faintly luminous, a living thing, with strength to overcome the fuggy stench of the dormitory. Sharp tang of rosemary, mustiness of rue, and odours Ellen did not recognise. She breathed it in. Her mind swirled, the scent sharpening her senses: the breaths of each inmate, the restlessness of their limbs, their mutterings and fartings.

Ellen's mind is jolted to the present by muffled sniggers from the crowd. Markey is telling his tale. His eyes are wild, his answers bumbling, incoherent. She frowns. The sniggers erupt into untrammelled laughter.

The clerk shouts for order. Markey glares at the spectators, at the clerk, at the magistrate. His eyes shift briefly to Ellen, and away again. He is told to return to his seat while others are called.

Others? More like Cooper? Is Ellen to go full circle?

The old woman in the grey nightgown had grinned a toothless grin. 'Tis a little magic,' she said. 'All is for buying, if you know how to pay.'

'Magic?' Heady, savouring the scents, Ellen shifted her gaze from the pouch to the baby, and back to the leathery face. 'Then why are you in this place, Mother?'

'For you.' The woman coughed, brought her free hand to her scrawny throat. 'Go on, have it.'

Ellen clasped the greasy calico. The crone shifted on the straw mattress, bade Ellen do the same, and touched foreheads across the gap. The murmur of secret words buzzed in Ellen's ears – incomprehensible, yet each one bearing meaning. Each sentence carrying new life. The baby, fretfully asleep in her arms, loosened a tiny fist from his swaddling and waved it. His mouth pursed, seeking food.

The crone's murmurings faded into a blankness broken by the baby bawling his demands in the early dawn. His cries were lusty, his weak mewling a thing of yesterday. Ellen's full breasts tingled, demanding their own satisfaction.

In the next cot, the old woman lay on her back, the blanket pulled to her chin. Her eyes were open, yet whatever she saw, it was not the cobwebbed rafters of the dormitory. Ellen felt for the pouch at her side, tucked it into the baby's blanket. The workhouse inmates, alerted by the mysterious way of these things, gathered around the wizened body. Their eyes were sombre, their lips trembled.

The same sombre eyes are borne by the townsfolk as they come forward to take the witness stand. The stifling, sweat-soaked air is trapped in Ellen's lungs. She grasps the dock railing to counter the tremulous failure of her legs.

Would she undo it? Would she refuse the pouch, the old crone's whispers?

If it pleases his honour, each witness asserts, he should know how Mother Hayward's herbs and potions have cured their coughs and rashes, how her wise counselling has helped solve life's dilemmas, how they respect her, how she does all this willingly, at no charge. Ellen slides her hand into the deep pocket of her skirt, touches the threadbare pouch, now black with age and long use. Her breath eases with each testament. Her aching fingers loosen their grip, and her legs steady.

The magistrate nods. Mother Hayward is no witch. She has no magic, simply skills and the experiences of a long life.

Ellen lifts her eyes, seeking her son, grown tall, robust. He stands at the back, ensuring she can see him. He tilts his head to the side, grins their secret across the heads of the crowd.

Based on the true story of Ellen Hayward, tried for witchcraft in the Forest of Dean, SW England, in 1906.

Many thanks to our first-round judges:
Karen Alvey
Miriam Fitzelle-Jones
Julia Hart
Jean Lang
Betty Moxon
Kate Jewell
Barbara Milner
Ned Palmer
Ellen Rawson
Imogen Robertson

And our final-round judges:
Janet Angelini
Matt Casbourne
Katherine Clements
Norah Perkins

Many congratulations to all the longlisted writers:
A Pact Fulfilled ~ Eleanor Swift-Hook
And an Axe ~ Hilary Orme
Annie's Sacred Pilgrimage ~ Sue du Feu
Ayla the Apothecary ~ Chris Cottom
Circles in the Sand ~ Sallyann Halstead
Cross to Bear ~ Laura Karim
Demons and Monkeys ~ Tamako Takamatsu
Deus ex Machina ~ Thea Burgess
Dividing Lines ~ Hilary Coyne
Hide and Seek ~ Maggie Richell-Davies
Liberty Coaster ~ Sierra Kaag
Loyalty ~ Victoria Blake
Maewyn's Day ~ Valerie Bowes

Terrible Beauty, Redux ~ HM Hulme
The Beheading Game ~ Nayani Jensen
The Great Jemima ~ Sarah Frances
The Telftbury Manikin ~ Valerie Thompson
Watch Out for Snakes ~ Terry Mulhern
Where the Wildflowers Grow ~ Mark Stewart

About the Dorothy Dunnett Society

Dorothy Dunnett relished her relationship with her readers, listening to their views and always replying to their letters. She set up the Dorothy Dunnett Society to help us to keep in touch with each other and to promote discussion and debate about history, literature and art, as well as her ever-fascinating characters, and in so doing helped create an international community of readers.

The Society has over 750 members around the world who receive *Whispering Gallery*, our quarterly magazine about all things Dunnett with articles about characters and sources, as well as the history and art of the times in which the books are set, together with fascinating extracts from Dorothy Dunnett's archive. The Society is also active on social media (Facebook, X and Instagram).

Dunnett readers around the world love nothing more than getting together to share their common interests in history, art, music and books. There is an annual Dunnett Weekend in Edinburgh and local gatherings in different places around the world. There have been organised journeys to favourite Dunnett location such as Malta, Venice and Istanbul and many, many individual and small group excursions. Each year we celebrate International Dorothy Dunnett Day on the second Saturday in November, when members meet in groups large and small with a celebratory glass raised at 1pm (local time).

2023 has been a special year for the Society as it marks the centenary of Dorothy Dunnett's birth. Over 270 delegates met in Edinburgh to attend Centenary celebrations, with a 2-day academic conference on the theme of Understanding Diversity in the 15th and 16th Centuries, our annual conference, and many trips, events and meals, together with a glorious concert of renaissance music in St Giles. The Society also created a special Centenary website <u>Dorothy Dunnett Centenary (dunnettcentral.org)</u>where you can read more about Dorothy Dunnett's life and work.

The Society also has its own shop where you can buy all sorts of splendid things, from mugs to the Dorothy Dunnett Guides to some of her locations: Istanbul, Bruges, Orkney and North-East Scotland, Iceland, Russia and Edinburgh are currently available from Amazon and in the shop on the Dorothy Dunnett Society website: <u>https://dunnettcentral.org</u>.

Many of Dorothy Dunnett's books are available as audiobooks on Audible – long and immersive reads.

Dorothy Dunnett's Books
The Lymond Chronicles

The Lymond Chronicles, six novels set in 16th-century Europe, follow the life and career of a Scottish nobleman, Francis Crawford of Lymond, at the time of the rough wooing. The adventure takes us from Scotland to France with the young Mary, to the defence of Malta against the Turks, to Istanbul, to Russia at the time of Ivan the Terrible, then, in the sixth book, back to France and Scotland. It's a wonderful sweeping tale in the tradition of Walter Scott – high drama, convoluted plotting, a cast of hundreds (most of them real historical figures), told with great attention to historical accuracy and a painterly eye for vivid description.

The volumes are *The Game of Kings* (1961), *Queens'*

Play (1964), *The Disorderly Knights* (1966), *Pawn in Frankincense* (1969), *The Ringed Castle* (1971), and *Checkmate* (1975).

King Hereafter

King Hereafter (1982), a stand-alone novel set in Orkney and Scotland in the 11th century, was, in Dorothy's eyes, her masterpiece. It is based on the premise that the central historical character Thorfinn, Earl of Orkney, and Macbeth, King of Alba, were one and the same person. King Hereafter was exhaustively researched and plunges the reader into battles, wild landscapes, political intrigue, cruelty, comedy, blood-shed, love and tragedy–and, above all, the formidable young king's relationship with the sea.

The House of Niccolò

The House of Niccolò comprises eight novels set in 15th-century Europe. The protagonist is Nicholas de Fleury (also known as Claes, Niccolò and Nicholas vander Poele), a dyer's apprentice from Bruges who climbs the mercantile ladder of Renaissance Europe taking in the wide sweep of European activity of that century in Italy and the Hanseatic League, Burgundy and Flanders, Poland, Muscovy and Iceland, the Black Sea cities of Trebizond and Caffa, Cyprus, Rhodes, Egypt and the Sinai Peninsula, West Africa, Timbuktu and the Sahara...and, of course, Scotland.

The volumes are *Niccolò Rising* (1986), *The Spring of the Ram* (1987), *Race of Scorpions* (1989), *Scales of Gold* (1991), *The Unicorn Hunt* (1993), *To Lie With Lions* (1995), *Caprice and Rondo* (1997), *Gemini* (2000).

Johnson Johnson

In addition to her major historical novels, Dorothy Dunnett wrote some lighter thrillers which were originally published under her maiden name of Dorothy Halliday and with various titles. They are now available from Farrago Press with splendidly stylish covers. They feature Johnson Johnson, a portrait painter with a yacht called Dolly and some of Dunnett's most splendid female characters as well as the expected exotic locations and much derring-do and humour. The titles are *Tropical Issue* (*Dolly and the Bird of Paradise*) 1983; *Rum Affair* (*Dolly and the Singing Bird*; *The Photogenic Soprano*) 1968; *Ibiza Surprise* (*Dolly and the Cookie Bird*; *Murder in the Round*) 1970; *Operation Nassau* (*Dolly and the Doctor Bird*; *Match for a Murderer*) 1971; *Roman Nights* (*Dolly and the Starry Bird*; *Murder in Focus*) 1973; *Split Code* (*Dolly and the Nanny Bird*) 1976; and *Moroccan Traffic* (*Send a Fax to the Kasbah*) 1991.

About the Historical Writers' Association

Our passion is history. We are authors, publishers, bloggers and agents of historical writing, both fiction and non-fiction, and we created the HWA to promote, support and connect our members, and to introduce readers to brilliant books. Whatever type of historical writing you are looking for you'll find HWA members are writing it. Wartime adventures, court intrigues, extraordinary explorations of ordinary lives, the swirl of social change and new perspectives on every aspect of our past, all bound up by superb story-telling. Our growing social media following allows readers and writers to connect and share their enthusiasms and interests as well as letting book buyers into the secret histories which lie behind every line our members write.

Historia is our online magazine for readers of historical fiction and non-fiction. Updated every week with reviews, feature articles, writing advice and interviews it has a dedicated audience and a growing list of subscribers. Regular giveaways, behind the scenes insights into the writing life and a fresh, modern voice make it the place to discover your new favourite author, find the next novel for your book group or find in-depth discussions of how and why we write what we do.

www.historiamag.com
www.historicalwriters.org

Printed in Great Britain
by Amazon

31735650R00056